INSCRIPTIONS

If the instinct to write one's name or leave one's mark on any available blank wall is not universal, it is at least very widespread all over Europe and in countries which have come under European influence. Greek mercenaries carved their names on the bases of the statues of Rameses II at Abu Simbel, the inhabitants of Pompeii scrawled their opinions on the walls of their town for archaeologists to find centuries later, the graffiti on medieval churches are being studied for the sake of the historical events they commemorate; nearer to our own time, Kilroy has left his mark throughout the modern world, and the walls near any bus stop and in every Underground station bear witness to the fact that it is still a living tradition. The only necessities seem to be time to kill, a suitable space and a writing implement. The results will vary according to the skill of the author, his education and interests and, especially, the time at his disposal; but results, it seems, there will be.

The various inhabitants of the Tower of London who have left their marks on its walls have certainly varied in their talents and interests, but whether prisoners or warders the one thing they have had in common has been time, and many of them have made good use of it. Some of the inscriptions are mere idle scratchings, but some are elaborate bas-relief carvings, some are moral reflections which perhaps served the dual purpose of occupying the carver's time and calming his spirits, and yet others are specific aids to devotion. Some tell something of their makers and why they were imprisoned; others are completely anonymous. There is nothing

to show which is the oldest of those still to be seen . . . should presumably . . . hed by the original . . . which were unc . . . ation of the Wakefie . . . pose however was utilitarian, . . . to while away the time, and they are really outside the scope of this study. Most of the inscriptions that can in any way be dated seem, not surprisingly, to be of the sixteenth and seventeenth centuries. This was the period when the use of the Tower as a whole was changing.

For the first few centuries of its existence the Tower was one of the strongest of the king's palaces, which, because of its geographical position in the administrative and commercial centre of the kingdom, acquired a character as a permanent government office and a state prison. During the sixteenth century its use as a royal residence was much diminished, and the phrase 'to be sent to the Tower' acquired a meaning synonymous with imprisonment on suspicion of treason. During the forties, the French ambassador wrote: 'When a man is a prisoner in the Tower none dare meddle with his affairs, unless to speak ill of him, for fear of being suspected of the same crime'. It should be emphasised however that even when its prison population was at its highest this was never the sole, nor even the prime, function of the Tower. It continued to house the Mint, some of the Crown Jewels and the growing organisation of the Office of Ordnance with its arsenal of armour and weapons and its workshops. All these were relics of the days when the Tower was the largest and strongest of the royal palaces and many of them remained long after its function as a prison had fallen into disuse. In addition, a large number of officials continued to live in it. Once the political stability associated with the mid-eighteenth century had succeeded to the upheavals of the seventeenth century, governments felt less need to imprison their opponents. In times of crisis, the Jacobite leaders of 1715 and 1745 or the Cato Street conspirators would be sent to the Tower, and individual opponents of the government like John Wilkes or of Parliament like Lord Mayor Crosby and Alderman Oliver might still spend a short sojourn therein, but most of the old prison rooms were adapted to more routine administrative or domestic uses, their walls were plastered over and the inscriptions left by their earlier inhabitants disappeared from sight.

On the 17th November 1796 however the Rev. John Brand, Secretary to the Society of Antiquaries of London, read to a meeting of that Society a paper which began:

'There is a room in Beauchamp's Tower, in the Tower of London, antiently the place of confinement for state prisoners, and which has lately been converted into a mess-room for the officers of the garrison there. On this alteration being made a great number of inscriptions was discovered on the walls of the room, which probably have, for the most part, been made with nails, and are all of them, it should seem, the undoubted autographs, at different periods, of the several illustrious and unfortunate tenants of this once dreary mansion.' ('An account of the inscriptions discovered on the walls of an appartment in the Tower of London', *Archaeologia* XIII (1800), pp 68–91).

He went on to describe some of the many inscriptions in the Beauchamp Tower, to give an account of a few of their authors and to make guesses at the possible origins of others. The printed version of his lecture was illustrated by engravings of scale drawings of most of the inscriptions he described, and it started a hunt for inscriptions and their authors which has gone on ever since. John Bayley, in his monumental *History and Antiquities of the Tower of London* published in 1825, not only corrected some of Brand's readings and attributions but also described some of the many inscriptions to be found in other parts of the Tower. His was the first study of the Tower of London to be based to any great extent on the Public Records, and the accuracy of much of his account is still unchallenged; moreover, his description of the Tower as it was just before the major Victorian rebuildings is of great interest for that reason alone. About thirty years later the Beauchamp Tower was in fact one of the first towers to receive an antiquarian restoration as distinct from a functional repair. The opportunity was then taken to record and preserve as many more inscriptions as could be found, and in 1851 a new series of lithographs with detailed descriptions was published by the Clerk of Works to Anthony Salvin, the architect in charge of the restorations (W. R. Dick,

Tower of London: a series of 31 lithographic plates illustrative of the inscriptions and devices in the Beauchamp Tower, with a short historical sketch of their authors). This was the last detailed study to be published devoted exclusively to the inscriptions, but they continued to be studied and recorded by the architects who were responsible for the upkeep of the Tower. By the time that the Report of the Royal Commission on Historical Monuments upon East London was published in 1930 its authors listed some 340 known inscriptions, and now, over forty years later, the Ancient Monuments Inspectorate of the Department of the Environment has distinguished more than 400. Rubbings and photographs have been made of nearly all of them, and the present booklet is based on this comprehensive record.

It has to be admitted that only a comparatively small proportion of the inscriptions has been completely elucidated, and it is highly unlikely that the authors of all of them will ever be identified. Large numbers are now illegible, and many are completely anonymous, consisting simply of a cross or the monogram IHS scratched on the wall. Others are simply a pair of initials with no other identifying signs. Even where these initials have a date attached

it is extremely difficult to be sure of an identification. Thus one may guess that the owners of the initials scratched in the White Tower in 1656 were opponents of Cromwell's policies, but the lists of prisoners and the lists of officials who served in the Tower are so incomplete that they may equally easily have been bored clerks or soldiers, for prisoners were not the only inmates to carve their names on the walls of the Tower. In 1605 a warder, William Underhill, wrote his name in the Byward Tower and took the trouble to scratch 'Wardr' after it. Little else is known about this man, but at least we know that at that time he was not a prisoner. Even some of the larger and more elaborate inscriptions have been left anonymous: one in the Bell Tower which consists of a verse beginning 'Bi torture straunge my trouth was tried' is unsigned, but the verse was well enough known for Thomas Miagh to quote it in one of his inscriptions dated 1581 in the Beauchamp Tower. Again T. Peverel, who carved his name and arms and several religious symbols and phrases in two places in the Beauchamp Tower in 1571, and T. Salmon, who included an exact accounting of the days of his imprisonment and a punning badge consisting of three fishes in his decoration of the walls of his prison in 1622, are apparently unknown both to history books and the Public Records. On the other hand the careers of the Dudley brothers are a part of English history, and something is known about the authors of many of the less elaborate carvings.

The prisoners who as a group have been most carefully studied are the religious martyrs of the sixteenth and early seventeenth centuries. The compilation known to most English-speaking Protestant homes for more than three centuries as Foxe's *Book of Martyrs* was put together by a man who had himself fled abroad to escape the Marian persecutions and it recounted the sufferings of men and women he had known or of whom he could still obtain accounts from those who had known them. The English Catholic recusants and the devoted

priests who came to minister to them have been the subjects of panegyrics and serious historical research since the time of their first sufferings, and historians of the Tower and its inscriptions have benefited greatly from the work of the historians of the Society of Jesus. Protestants who suffered for their faith were imprisoned in the Tower less frequently than Catholics and certainly left fewer recognisable inscriptions. As a general rule, the Protestants' crime was considered a religious one to be tried in the bishops' courts and only punished by the civil authorities, but Catholics were considered potential traitors by the mere fact of their faith. Hence, ordinary Protestants were imprisoned in the bishop's own prisons unless they had actually been involved in treasonable conspiracies, while Catholics were often kept and questioned in those of the State.

Treason or potential treason in its widest sense was the usual pretext for imprisonment in the Tower, although there were exceptions, and many of the identified authors of inscriptions were implicated in the various conspiracies and rebellions that marked the Tudor period. The first large batch of dated inscriptions, those of 1537, can be associated with the unrest after the Pilgrimage of Grace while another group in the White Tower includes those of some of the men imprisoned after Wyatt's rebellion of 1553-4. There are names associated with the Ridolfi and Babington plots against the life of Queen Elizabeth in 1571 and 1586 and the name occurs of Elizabeth's own Italian tutor imprisoned along with other members of her household by Queen Mary in 1556. The sons of the Duke of Northumberland spent much of Queen Mary's reign in the Tower after the failure of their father's attempt to set Lady Jane Grey on the throne, and Arthur and Edmund Pole died in the Tower seven years after the discovery of their inept attempt to ensure the succession of Mary Queen of Scots. Lastly there are two of the Gunpowder Plot conspirators.

The inscriptions are not distributed evenly through the Tower. They have so far been found in the following places: Beauchamp Tower (more than 95), North and South Byward Towers (33), Bloody Tower (28), Broad Arrow Tower (26), Martin Tower (29), North and South Middle Towers (9), St. Thomas's Tower (3), Salt Tower (55), Wakefield Tower (2) and Well Tower (9); in the White Tower (89), and Queen's House and the Bell Tower (10). Apart from the two Byward Towers, which presumably must normally have housed a guard, most have been found in the Beauchamp, Bloody, Broad Arrow, Martin and Salt Towers, and the White Tower. This may to a large extent be the result of the vagaries of rebuilding and restoration, for some towers were demolished in the eighteenth century and others almost completely rebuilt during the nineteenth. Even so, it suggests that some towers were more used as prisons than others, and this suggestion is in part confirmed by a document in the British Library: a 'Perticular of the names of the

Towers and Prison Lodgings in his majesty's Tower of London, taken out of a paper of Mr. William Franklyns, sometyme Yeoman Warder, dat. 16th March, 1641 . . .' lists the various towers in order and gives a brief note about the appropriation of each one (Harl. Ms. 1326). After noting that the White Tower was then devoted to the needs of the Office of Ordnance, it continues:

Cradle Tower A prison lodging . . .
Well Tower A prison lodging . . .
Salt Tower At the end of the long gallery, a prison lodging.
Broad Arrow Tower upon the wall by the king's garden, a prison lodging.
Constable Tower betwixt capt. Coningsby and Mr. Marsh, a prison lodging.
Martin Tower, over against the green Mount, near Mr. Sherburn's house, a prison lodging . . .
Beauchamp Tower or *Cobham Tower*, betwixt the chapel and the Lts. lodging, a prison lodging.

Bell Tower Adjoyning to the lts. house, a prison lodging.

Wakefield Tower or *Bluddy Tower* Against the Watergate, a prison lodging . . .

Nunn's Bower The prisons over Coleharbour Gate.

Lanthorne Tower Parte of the kings lodgings, under wch is a prisoners lodging, wth a dore next to the lowe gardens.'

The Lanthorn Tower was completely rebuilt in the middle of the last century, the Cradle and Constable Towers were heavily restored at the same time, and the Coldharbour Gate was demolished in the seventeenth century, but otherwise the two lists coincide to a remarkable degree. These towers were in fact the Tower of London's famous, or infamous, dungeons, unpleasant enough no doubt, but hardly as noisome as popular imagination or hostile propaganda has sometimes painted them.

As has been implied earlier, there are no complete lists of all the prisoners who have at one time or another been immured in the Tower. There are three main sources of information concerning the identity of the owners of the names scratched on the Tower's walls. The more important or dangerous appear both in contemporary chronicles and diaries, in the State Papers in the Public Record Office, which often contain accounts of the arrest, interrogation, trial and sometimes execution of those who were considered a danger to the State, and in the surviving records of the actual trials themselves, when, as was not always the case, the suspected traitors were in fact brought to trial. Less important men sometimes received a passing mention in the chronicles or appeared in one of the occasional returns of prisoners, with the reasons for their imprisonment, which were sometimes demanded from the Lieutenant of the Tower. Finally, prisoners who were supported by the Government were listed in the Lieutenant's quarterly accounts along with the money necessary for the Lieutenant's own fee and the wages of the Yeoman Warders. The records do not make it absolutely clear when a prisoner was expected to support himself and when he could receive one of the varying rates of official 'diet'. Personal wealth was of course one criterion, but it is not clear that it was the only one: after attainder or condemnation for treason a prisoner was apparently supported at government expense, presumably because his property was now forfeit to the Crown. What is certain is that a gentleman was better fed than a commoner and a nobleman fed best of all. During the sixth year of the reign of Edward VI (1552–3), the then Lieutenant, Sir Arthur Darcie, accounted for sums of 100s. a week, and the keep of four servants for the maintenance of the Duke of Somerset, while ordinary gentlemen were fed for 20s. a week and commoners for 5s. plus 2s. 6d. weekly for 'fewel and candle'. The rate of inflation in the sixteenth century brought some rise in these rates: by the end of the century the minimum rate had gone up to 6s. 8d. with 2s. 6d. for fuel and candle, while 13s. 4d. with 4s. for fuel and candle was more usual. Some of the names which appear on the walls of the Tower however seem to appear in none of these sources of information, even though the form of the inscription makes it reasonably certain that they are in fact those of prisoners. We can only speculate as to the reason for the sojourn in the Tower thus commemorated.

It has not been possible in the space available in this essay to do more than comment on a few of the inscriptions which have survived. The accompanying illustrations offer only a selection of the more interesting: some are in towers usually open to the public, and others are in buildings which are either lived in or being used as administrative offices, or are undergoing restoration and can only be visited, if at all, by special prior arrangement.

SARAH BARTER

Opposite: John Dudley's inscription. See page 15

IOH·N DVDLE

YOW THAT THESE BEASTS DO WEL BEHOLD AND SE
MAY DEME WITH EASE WHERFORE HERE MADE THEY BE
WITH BORDERS EKE WHERIN
4 BROTHERS NAMES WHO LIST TO SERCHE THE GROVND

Masons' marks Wakefield Tower

Two masons' marks discovered during the recent restoration of the Wakefield Tower.

Much has been written about masons' marks, but their exact significance is still somewhat obscure. In some places, for instance Torgau on the river Elbe, an apprentice was assigned a mark by his master if he was forced to travel independently to find work before his training was complete. There is apparently no evidence of a similar system at work in England and L. F. Salzman comments:

'Whether marks were assigned in the same way in England or merely assumed is not known. Their practical purpose must have been to identify the work of the individual mason for the information of the paymaster. It is noticeable that these marks rarely appear on tracery or carved stone, most of which . . . would be easily identified. That they usually appear on only a portion, often quite a small proportion, of the plain stones of a building suggests that they may have applied only to the men who were on piece work, or possibly to the casual labourers who were not known to the master and whose work it was therefore desirable to check'. (*Building in England down to 1540*, Oxford 1952, p 127)

Whatever the exact circumstances in which they were used, they apparently became closely associated with their owners, and there are examples of their being used to attest documents.

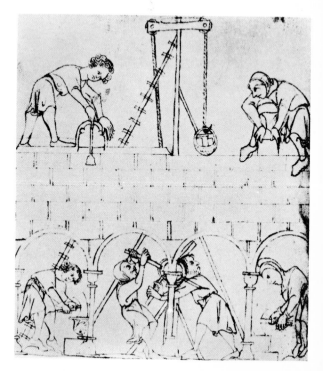

Underhill; Waad; crossbow and bolt

Byward Tower

'Will Underhill Wardr 1605'

'Ezechiell Waad Warder'

These inscriptions are to be found in the Byward
Tower. William Underhill is recorded in the Roll of
Yeoman Warders of the Tower as having joined in
1605, but of Ezechiell Waad no record has been
found at that or any other date. The guards in the
Tower were as likely to have time to kill as their
prisoners. In another tower, the Salt Tower, Michael
Moody, who was imprisoned from 15 January
1586–7 until at least July 1588 for 'practising with
the ffrench ambassador' has carved his name, and
in the same room appears the inscription
'Edwardus Hyrste 1587 January 24 custos MM hoc
scripsit', usually interpreted as 'Edward Hyrste . . .
keeper of Michael Moody wrote this'.

The crossbow and its bolt are presumably the sort
of thing a bored guard might well decide to scratch
on an empty piece of wall: something that was easy
to outline and frequently to be seen in such a military
establishment as the Tower has always been.

Beauchamp Tower

The 'room' in 'Beauchamp's Tower, in the Tower
of London, antiently the place of confinement for
state prisoners, . . . which has lately been converted
into a mess-room for the officers of the garrison
there', as it was illustrated in 1796 in Volume XIII
of *Archaeologia*. About 1850 this tower was the first
to undergo a thorough restoration under the
supervision of the architect Anthony Salvin. The
work was completed and the room with its inscriptions
was opened to the public in 1854. It is still the one
room in the Beauchamp Tower open to the public.
The engraving is clear enough for it to be possible to
identify most of the inscriptions shown. Those of the
Earl of Arundel and of the Dudley Brothers (see pages
28 and 15) are particularly obvious, but one of Charles
Bailly's two inscriptions (see page 22) can also be

seen in the embrasure to the far right of the picture,
and the horse-shoe surrounding one of Thomas
Peverell's inscriptions can be seen in the next bay,
with above it the outline, apparently copied from
the Bailly inscription, of Thomas Clarke's
inscription dated 1576.

Some idea of the accommodation provided, at
least in the late seventeenth century, can be gathered
from a report by Sir Christopher Wren dated
17 April 1695:
'In obedience to yr. Lrs. order of the 15th instant,
that I should view . . . Beauchamp Tower and ye
Bloody Tower and report wt. Expense will put them
in condition to hold prisoners of State and what
number they will hold I have accordingly viewed
the same and report that both the said places were
put the last summer in better repair than they have

been in many years being whited mended and made
strong, but to make them fitt for prisoners of State,
if by that Expression it be intended that they should
be wainscotted and made fitt for hangings and
furniture it may cost £200 or much more but with
such walls, windows and winding stairs they never
can be made proper with any cost without rebuilding
... As to the number of Prisoners the place may hold
I can only report wt. number of rooms each place
contains. Beauchamp Tower hath a large kitching
2 large rooms and 2 small servants rooms. Bloody
Tower hath a kitching one room and one closet . . . .'
(quoted R. Sutherland Gower, *Tower of London*,
London 1902, II p 94).

The rebus of Thomas Abel
Beauchamp Tower
Thomas Abel was a distinguished doctor of divinity
who was also a good musician and linguist. He
attracted the notice of Henry VIII and his then
queen, Katherine of Aragon, and was appointed the
Queen's domestic chaplain about 1528. In the
interminable arguments about the royal divorce, he
took the queen's side; he was instrumental in
persuading the Emperor Charles V to continue to
refuse it his recognition and he himself wrote a book
giving the queen's side of the argument, *Invicta
veritas . . . tractatus de non desolvendo Henrici et
Catherinae matrimonio* (1532). When Henry's marriage
to Anne Boleyn was finally made public, Abel was
one of those who refused to recognise the change in
his mistress's position. He declared that for any of
her servants, if they had once sworn to serve her as
queen, to serve her giving her the title of 'Princess
Dowager' which had been officially accorded to her
would be tantamount to perjury. Among the State
Papers in the Public Record Office is a letter, dated
19 December 1533, reporting this judgement and
another of 27 December reporting his imprisonment.
He spent altogether about five and a half years in
the Tower. In the spring of 1537, he wrote a sad

letter to Thomas Cromwell, then Lord Privy Seal
and the King's most influential minister, saying:
'I have now been in close prison three years and a
quarter come Easter', and begging to be allowed to
go out to Church and 'to lie in some house upon the
Green'. Another document in the British Library
notes that it cost 40d. a week to support him in
prison. In 1540 Parliament finally passed a bill of
attainder against him and several others 'who have
refused the King's supremacy'. He and two other
Catholic priests were hanged at Tyburn on 30 July
1540; ironically enough this was two days after
Thomas Cromwell, by then Earl of Essex and Lord
Great Chamberlain, had been beheaded for high
treason and at the same time as three Protestant
preachers were burned for heresy.

Sedbar Beauchamp Tower

'Adam Sedbar Abbas Jorevallis 1537'

Adam Sedbar was, as he proclaims, abbot of the monastery of Jervaulx, in Yorkshire; he was in fact the eighteenth, and last, abbot of one of the most important Cistercian abbeys in the country. He was arrested early in 1537 under suspicion of involvement in the so-called Pilgrimage of Grace, a series of risings against the government centred on Lincolnshire and the North. They are said to have started in protest against the increasingly rapid dissolution of religious houses, but seem to have had a solid foundation of economic, social and political grievances to lend support. The risings were put down without much difficulty and, whatever their fundamental causes, one of the results of their failure was the arrest for treasonable activities of the heads of many of the larger Northern abbeys. Adam

Sedbar himself was questioned in the Tower on 25 April 1537 and confessed to giving the rebels some very limited aid, he claimed under duress. This confession was made the basis of the indictment at his trial when with others he was accused of plotting 'as false traitours to deprive the king of his title of Supreme Head of the English Church, and to compel him to hold a certain Parliament and convocation of the clergy of the realm'. They were tried and condemned on 14th, 15th and 16th May and a letter preserved in the Public Record Office, dated 'Trinity even', that is 26 May 1537, described his execution at Tyburn on 'the Friday in Whitsun week'.

There are at least three other inscriptions in the Beauchamp Tower made by prisoners involved in these uprisings, those of Ravlef (Ralph) Bulmer, George Ardern and Ingram Percy.

Anon. Beauchamp Tower
'*I C*'; '*Lerne to feare God I C 1538*'

Two of the three inscriptions left by I C (or C I) in
the Beauchamp Tower. The third reads *Reprens le
sage et il te aymera* (Return to the good and it will love
you). There is no certain way of identifying I C: he
is one of many, though an exceptionally skilled
executant, who carved their initials on the walls of
their prisons and left no other indication of who they
were or why they were there.

It is just possible, given the date and the sentiments
expressed, that I C was John Collins, a priest in the
service of Henry Pole, Lord Montague. Montague
was committed to the Tower in 1538, accused of
denying Henry VIII's title of Supreme Head of the
Church of England, and was finally executed 9
December 1538. Collins was imprisoned at the same
time as his master, was delivered for trial 4 December
1538, entered a plea of guilty and was condemned to
execution at Tyburn. A mid-sixteenth century
manuscript list of 'men executed in Hen. 8 times',
now in the British Library (Titus B 1 f.136), notes
succinctly: 'Collyns preste At Tiburne 9 Jan. 1538',
that is in January 1539 by the modern calendar, a
month after his master.

Jane Grey Beauchamp Tower
'Iane'

This inscription is traditionally associated with Lady Jane Grey. The first enthusiastic account by the Reverend John Brand firmly claimed that it was carved by the unfortunate lady herself, but as John Bayley in his more accurately documented description rather stuffily remarked 'The ... idea, to which the repetition of the word *Jane* has given rise, is not borne out by history ... for, however severe might formerly have been the treatment of state delinquents, a sense of delicacy seems always to have been preserved towards the weaker sex; and when a

female of distinction had the misfortune to be committed to the Tower, she was usually confined in the private house of the lieutenant, or some other respectable officer of the fortress' (*History of the Tower of London*, I p 162). He went on to point out that as the famous carving of the bear and ragged staff showed that at least some of the Dudley brothers were imprisoned in that particular room of the Beauchamp Tower, it was highly unlikely that Lady Jane would have been kept in the same room and put forward the suggestion, now generally accepted, that it was cut by her husband, Guildford Dudley, who was imprisoned at the same time and executed on the same day. According to Foxe's *Book of Martyrs*, Lady Jane is in fact supposed to have used a pin to scratch a Latin text on the wall of her room and to have signed it 'Jane Dudley'. 'The most diligent search, however, in every part of the Tower, to discover this interesting autograph, has proved fruitless; which, considering the lapse of years, and the very slight manner in which it must necessarily have been made, cannot be a matter of surprise' (Bayley, I pp 162–3). Lady Jane was in fact, as Bayley surmised, imprisoned in the lodgings of the Gentleman Gaoler on Tower Green. She was allowed to walk in the Lieutenant's Gardens and on the hill within the Tower and seems to have dined regularly with the Lieutenant himself. She and her husband and father and brothers-in-law were imprisoned at the end of July 1553. Northumberland was executed in August, but Lady Jane and her husband were not brought to trial until after Queen Mary's coronation in November and were not actually executed until the unrest manifested in Wyatt's rebellion had caused the Queen and her Council to feel insecure enough to want rival claimants to the throne out of the way. Attempts were made to persuade them to renounce their Protestant convictions and when these had failed they were finally executed, Lord Guildford on Tower Hill and Lady Jane herself more privately on Tower Green.

Dudley Beauchamp Tower

'*John Dudli*
Yow that these beasts do wel behold and se
May deme with ease wherefore here made they be
Withe borders eke wherein [there may be found]
4 Brothers names who list to serche the grounde.'
This, shown opposite page 6, is one of the most
elaborate and accomplished of the inscriptions in the
Tower. It shows a device consisting of the bear and
ragged staff, which had been the badge of the Earls
of Warwick at least since the 14th century and by
tradition since Saxon times, with the lion with two
tails which appeared in the Dudley family arms.
This is surrounded by a border of roses, gillyflowers,
oakleaves and honeysuckle. The verse beneath, which
is usually completed as it has been at the beginning
of this account, implies that the border symbolises
the names of four brothers, so the roses are usually
interpreted as standing for Ambrose, the
gillyflowers, probably clove carnations at this time,
for Guilford, the oakleaves for Robert – from *robur*,
Latin for oak – and the honeysuckle for Henry.
These were the names of the four brothers of John

Dudley, who were imprisoned with him in 1553–4
when the attempt of their father, John Dudley, Duke
of Northumberland and Earl of Warwick, to place
Lady Jane Grey on the throne had failed (see above).
Another inscription showing an oak branch and the
initials R D is attributed to Robert Dudley.
All five brothers were condemned as traitors in 1553,
but after Guilford's execution the other four were
reprieved and finally pardoned in the following
year. John Dudley, the eldest son, who bore the
courtesy title of Earl of Warwick during his father's
lifetime, died 21 October 1554, ten days after his
release from the Tower. The next brother, Ambrose,
eventually acceded to the title of Earl of Warwick
and became Master of the Ordnance to Queen
Elizabeth. Robert became Queen Elizabeth's
favourite and was created Earl of Leicester. Henry,
the youngest, was killed at the siege of St. Quentin,
10 August 1557, to which all three surviving brothers
had gone with the contingent of English troops sent
to support the Spanish besiegers, in an attempt to
regain the favour of Queen Mary and her husband
Philip II of Spain.

15

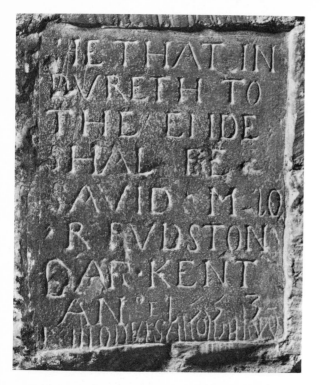

Rudston; Culpepper White Tower
'*He that indureth to the ende shal be savid. M.10.*
R. Rudston Dar. Kent An 1553.'
'*Be faithful unto the deth and I will give the a crowne of*
life. D(   ) 1554. DTL Culpepper of Ailsford Kent'.
These, which are both to be seen in the crypt of the
Chapel of St John in the White Tower, are
inscriptions left by associates of Sir Thomas Wyatt,
who in January 1553–4 led a body of Kentish
followers against London. He was later claimed as a
Protestant champion, but seems primarily to have
been stung into rebellion by Queen Mary's intention
of marrying the Spanish prince, who became King
Philip II of Spain. The Kentish men found first
London Bridge and then Ludgate defended against
their attacks and surrendered to the Earl of Pembroke
leading the royal troops on the night of 7–8 February.
This rebellion was made the pretext for the execution
of Lady Jane Grey and her husband Lord Guildford
Dudley, and attempts were made at Wyatt's trial
and after to make him implicate the Queen's sister,
the Princess Elizabeth. This he refused to do and he
was finally executed on 11th April 1554.

Both Robert Rudston and Thomas Culpepper were
brought to the Tower 8 February 1554, tried and
condemned at Westminster on 13 February, but
both, like the majority of Wyatt's followers, were
eventually pardoned and released in return for a
heavy fine. Rudstone was reprieved 18 March 1554
and pardoned 1 April while Culpepper had to wait
until 5 April for his pardon. Both failed to complete
payment of their fines before the end of Mary's reign
and were discharged of further payments during the
reign of Elizabeth.

Castiglione Broad Arrow Tower, Salt Tower

'In queste vanita ch'ogn'un desia
Non poner tua speranza ma sicure
Scorgi il camin ch'al sommo ben t'invia
Giovanni Battista Castiglione 1556'

(Do not rest your hopes on these vain things that all
men desire, but follow the sure road which leads to
the highest good).

The author of this exceptionally clear cut inscription
is usually identified as the Italian tutor of Princess
Elizabeth, later Queen Elizabeth I. John Baptist
Castiglione, a great-grandson of the author of the
famous book on the behaviour of a gentleman, *The
Courtier*, entered the service first of Henry VIII and
then of his younger daughter, married Margaret
Campayne (Compagno), the daughter of another
Italian immigrant, later 'mother of the maids of
honour' to the Queen, and founded the family of
Castillion which was settled at Benham Valence in
Berkshire during the 17th and 18th centuries. He is
known to have been twice imprisoned as a result of
Queen Mary's suspicions of her sister and her
sister's household at the time of two successive
Protestant uprisings, the Wyatt rebellion of 1553,
and the conspiracy of 1555–6 in which Sir John
Cheke and Sir Peter Carew were involved.

It would perhaps be romantic, but not wholly
unreasonable, to associate with the second period of
his imprisonment, when the Princess's household
rather than she herself was involved, not only the
inscription quoted above, but also another
inscription, in the Salt Tower, which consists of a
letter E, perhaps for Elizabeth, surrounded by the
outline of a heart, with the date *1556 Augusti 14*
above and the names *John Baptiste, Cristofer Per*
and *Cristofer Norton* beneath it. Christopher Norton
was involved in the 1571 Ridolfi plot, but a
Christopher Perne was arrested in 1556 and the
date, script and style of the inscription, and perhaps
the Italianate spelling of Christopher, make it
possible that it too was cut by Castiglione.

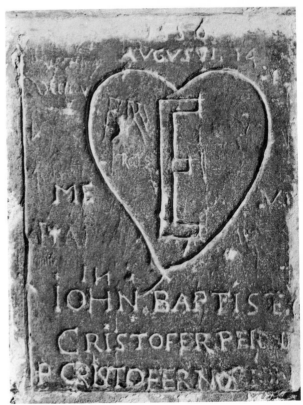

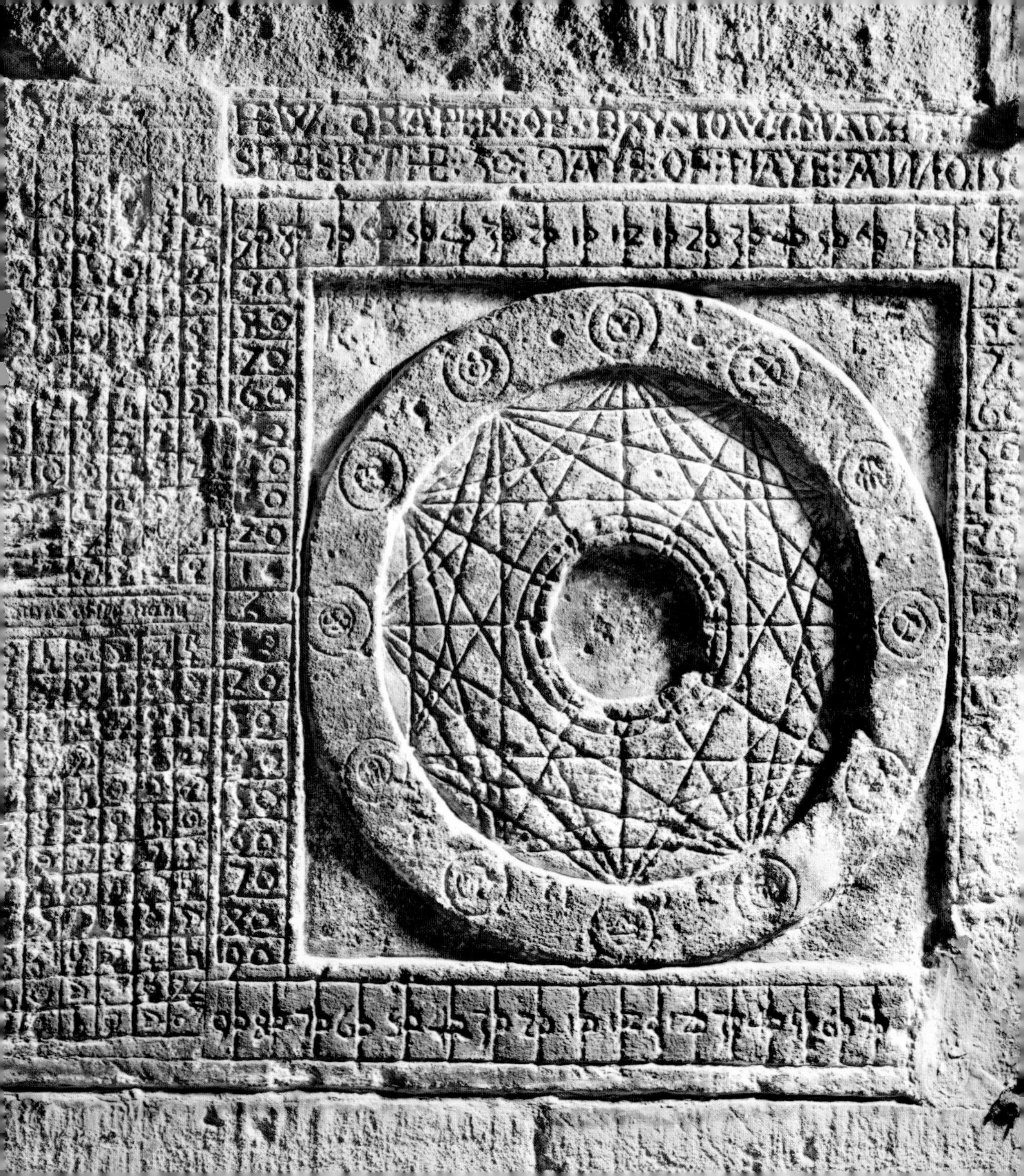

Draper Salt Tower

'Hew Draper of Brystow made thys spheer the 30 daye of Maye Anno 1561'

A diagram showing the signs of the zodiac with tables, presumably to be used in astrological forecasts. Hugh Draper of Bristol was imprisoned on suspicion of conspiring to use magic to harm Sir William or Lady St Loe who had estates at Tormarton near Bristol.

In a list of 'the names of the prisoners in the Tower, with the causes of their imprisonment, briefly set forthe, and delivered by Sir Edwarde Warner, knight lieutenant of ye said Tower to ye Lords of ye Quenes privie counsell, the 26th of May 1561', is the following entry:

'Hugh Draper, co'mitted the 21st of March, 1560. This man was brought in by the accusation of one John Man, an astronomer, as a suspect of a conjurer or sorcerer, and thereby to practise matter against Sr William St Lowe, and my ladie; and in his confession it aperithe, that before Time he hathe been busie and doinge wt suche matters; but he denieth any matter of weight touching Sr William Sentlo, or my ladie, and alsoe affirmethe yt longe since he so misliked his science, that he burned all

his bookes. He is presently verie sick: he semithe to be a man of good wealthe and kepithe a Tavern in Bristowe, and is of his neighbours well reported'. (Bayley, II pp l–li.)

Nothing much else is known about the unhappy Hugh Draper, except that he was not listed as a prisoner in March 1562. In 1561–2 there were at least two other men, Francis Cox and Ralph Davis, or Davison, imprisoned in the Tower, in connection with the same episode. The first was found guilty of 'conjuring', the second was 'supposed to be privy of the poisonings of my lady Seintlowe' but was soon set at liberty 'upon sureties'. 'My lady Seintlowe' was the lady known as Bess of Hardwicke, later Countess of Shrewsbury, who was at that time married to her third husband, Sir William St. Loe, the captain of the Queen's guard. Both Sir William and his wife knew the inside of the Tower's prisons; Sir William had been imprisoned for nearly a year in 1553 for suspicion of complicity with the Wyatt rebellion while Lady St. Loe was to spend nearly the same amount of time in the Tower later in 1561 as a suspected confidant of Lady Catherine Grey whose unauthorised marriage to the Earl of Hertford was discovered in August.

Poole Beauchamp Tower

'*Deo servire, penitentiam inire, fato obedire, regnare est.*
A. Poole 1564'

(To serve God, to endure penance, to obey fate, is to reign).

This is one of some half dozen inscriptions left in the Beauchamp Tower and elsewhere by the brothers Arthur and Edmund Poole or Pole. They were the grandchildren of that Duke of Clarence whose main claim to fame is his supposed death in a butt of malmsey wine. As a result of their Plantagenet descent, they inevitably became involved in one of the many plots against Queen Elizabeth, whose claim to the throne was so vulnerable to attacks from Yorkist legitimists and Catholic enthusiasts. According to the indictment of 22 February 1562–3 they were involved in a conspiracy to flee to France, proclaim Arthur Duke of Clarence and then return with an army of 5,000 men 'from the . . . duke of Guyse; and with the same armye in Maye next after, to arrive in Wales, and there to proclaim the . . . Skottyshe queen to be queen of England'. The Pooles and their accomplices explained in mitigation that they had been misled by one of the conspirators who had claimed to look into the future and had foretold the death of Queen Elizabeth within the year: they had not intended to put their plot into execution during the queen's lifetime. This plea was accepted, to the extent that no one was executed for high treason, but the Poole brothers spent the rest of their lives in prison. Both brothers left inscriptions dating from several periods of their lives on the walls of the Beauchamp Tower, and Edmund also left his mark in the Salt Tower in 1567. The exact date of their deaths is not known: they were both alive in January 1570, but are not mentioned in their mother's will which is dated 12 August 1570. The burial register of the chapel of St Peter ad Vincula was very inadequately kept at this time: it was recopied about 1587 and the copyist simply grouped the entries for the years between 1565 and 1578, which include:

'Mr. Arthur Poole's Brother buried in the chapel'
'Arthur Poole, buried in the chapel.'

Anon. Queen's House

'*As God preserved Christ his sone/*
In trouble and in thrall/
So when we call up on the Lord/
He will preserve us all./
Up on the twenty daie of Iune/in the yere of our Lord a
thousande/five hundred Thre scor and five was/the right
honorable countes of/Lennox grace commytede prysner/to
thys logynge for the marege/of her sonne my Lord Henry
Darnle/and the Quene of Scotlande/Here is there nams that
do wayte/up on her nobl grace in thys plase./M. Elizabeth
Husey/M. Ihan Baily/M. Elisabeth Chambalen/M.
Roberte Portyngton/Edwarde Cueyne/Anno Domini 1566.'
This inscription, above a fireplace in Queen's
House, was discovered when alterations and repairs
were being made during the 1820s and was first
described by James Markland FSA in a paper read
to the Society of Antiquaries on 25 February 1830
(*Archaeologia* XXXIII, 1831). It claims to
commemorate the imprisonment of Margaret
Countess of Lennox for conniving at the marriage of

her son with Mary Queen of Scots. She was a
granddaughter of Henry VII, niece to Henry VIII
and cousin of Queen Elizabeth I, and her whole life
was coloured by her proximity to the throne and her
Catholic faith. She was first imprisoned for
attempting to marry against the wishes of Henry
VIII; her second period of imprisonment was
occasioned by suspicions that she was plotting with
Mary Queen of Scots in the Catholic interest and
her third when she brought off the coup of marrying
her son to the Queen. She was imprisoned for about
eight months on this occasion, being released on 22
February 1566. She broke with Queen Mary,
naturally enough, when Darnley was killed in an
explosion at Kirk o'Field outside Edinburgh in 1567
but seems to have become reconciled to her before
her own death in 1578.

Bailly Beauchamp Tower

Principium Sapientie Timor Domini
(The fear of the Lord is the beginning of wisdom)
I.H.S. X.P.S. Anno D. 1571 10 September.
The most unhappy man in the world is he that is not
pacient in adversities. For men are not killed with the
adversities they have but with ye impacience which
they suffer.
'*Tout vient apoient quy peut attendre.*
(Everything comes aright to him who can wait)
Gli sospiri ne son testimoni veri dell'angoscia mia.
(Sighs are the true testimony of my anguish)
Aet. 29 Charles Bailly
Be enemye to none.
Be frend to one.
Hoependes Hert Pacientie'
(Hoping heart, patience).

Charles Bailly, 1542–1625, was a Fleming of Scottish descent who was at one time a member of the household of Mary Queen of Scots and who, after her imprisonment, became involved in the plot to murder Elizabeth and set Mary on the throne which was evolved by the Florentine banker Roberto Ridolfi. Bailly was arrested when he landed at Dover carrying letters in cipher addressed to the Queen of Scots and several of her English adherents. Although the letters were indecipherable at first, he was induced by various means, including, according to his own tale, the rack and promises of release with honour, to tell all that he knew about the conspiracy. The details of the intrigue were gradually unravelled by Elizabeth's Council, and the Duke of Norfolk and John Leslie, Bishop of Rosse, the Scottish ambassador, were both arrested, along with several of their adherents. Norfolk was eventually executed after much hesitation on the Queen's part but Bailly and Rosse were both released some time in 1573 and in 1574 Bailly is mentioned as being in Antwerp. He died in 1625 and was buried near Brussels where his tomb was to be seen as late as the end of the 19th century.

Charles Bailly is one of the few of the many prisoners in the Tower whose place of imprisonment is to some extent described in the meagre surviving day-to-day administrative records of the Tower as well as in the State Papers. In January 1571-2, the then Lieutenant of the Tower, Sir Owen Hopton, described the care he took of the prisoners in his charge when claiming expenses for their keep. He mentioned in passing that 'The under gaylor being a very trustie man, kepeth Hussye, Norton, Bates, Wylkinson, and Byshope, Cantrell, Hall, and Charles Baylie in Colherborowe' and claimed the sum of £8.18.8 for the support of 'Balye' for the period 27 April to 21 June 1571. By September Bailly had obviously been moved to the Beauchamp Tower where he had in fact been earlier as is proved by another inscription there dated 1570.

Anon. Bell Tower
Miagh Beauchamp Tower

'*Bi torture straunge/My trouth was tried/Yet of my libertie den/ied/*
Therfor reson hath/Me perswadyd that/Pasyens must be ymb/rasyd thogh hard/
Fortun chasyth/Me wyth smart/Yet pasyens shal pre/vail.'

This is a completely anonymous inscription in the Bell Tower, with nothing to indicate its probable date. The only rather curious connection found, which does at least provide a *terminus ad quem*, is with an inscription in the Beauchamp Tower, dated 1581. This is one of several signed by an Irishman, Thomas Miagh, who was sent to the Tower on suspicion of being implicated in one of the continuous series of rebellions which marked Elizabethan rule in Ireland. He was committed to the Tower in March 1580–1 and was examined in secrecy, being tortured, according to a report made to Sir Francis Walsingham, twice with Skevingtons Irons and later, in July 1581, when he had refused to reveal what he was supposed to know, with the rack. He had good reason to carve on the wall of his prison:

'*Thomas Miagh which lieth here alon*
That fayne would from hens be gon
By torture straunge mi trouth was tryed
Yet of my libertie denied 1581 Thomas Myagh'

In view of his fondness for carving his name, it seems unlikely that Miagh was responsible for the Bell Tower inscription, so it must be assumed either that the rhyme was current in the Tower at the time or that Miagh saw it during his stay in the Tower. As it is carved at the entrance to the uppermost room in the Bell Tower, it seems probable that he was imprisoned there, possibly during his first interrogation. Prisoners were often interrogated in the Lieutenant's Lodgings, now Queen's House, and there was an unsubstantiated legend of an underground passage leading from the building to the torture chamber in the basement of the White Tower. Miagh's interrogation seems to have been inconclusive: he was never brought to trial but was kept in the Tower until the summer of 1583, although he had been allowed the 'liberty of the Tower' as early as November 1581. This meant that he could move freely about within the Tower precincts, rather than being kept 'close prisoner' in his cell.

Stapleton Bloody Tower

'Sana Conscientia Murus Henricus Stapleton 20 Nov. 1583'

(A healthy conscience is a defence).

In spite of the fact that it is apparently signed and dated, the author of this inscription is not definitely known. The only Stapleton who has been traced as being in the Tower at this date is Sir Robert Stapleton of Wighill in Yorkshire who was imprisoned during part of 1583 and 1584 for his part in an attempt to blackmail the then Archbishop of York. He was certainly in the Tower between August and December 1583, when he petitioned Burleigh, as Lord Treasurer, for the relative freedom of the 'liberty of the Tower' because his health had suffered 'with long restraint in prisons close and unwholesome'. He was apparently transferred at some time after this to the Fleet prison whence he again petitioned for release in May 1584. It has been suggested that Henry Stapleton was a member of another branch of the same family, who were notorious Catholics and hence liable to imprisonment under suspicion of treason at any time by the simple fact of their religion. However, the only Henry Stapleton who has been traced as being alive at that date was the eldest son of the Sir Robert Stapleton who was imprisoned, who was 25 in 1599 and would therefore have been only about 9 or 10 in 1583 (H. E. Chetwynd-Stapylton *The Stapeltons of Yorkshire*, London 1897, pp 225–35). There is no indication that he was ever imprisoned with his father and this would have been most unlikely in view of the crime involved, although it was occasionally done in cases of treason or suspected treason.

Anon. Beauchamp Tower

Another elaborate, but inelegant, carving which is yet again anonymous. It apparently shows a man kneeling at an altar, although it has been suggested that it depicts a prisoner in the notorious 'Little Ease' prison in which the victim could not stand, sit or lie at ease. It is associated with a crudely cut inscription 'Vincet qui patitur Ro. Baynbrige' (He conquers who endures) but it is not clear whether the two belong together. Nothing definite is known of Robert Baynbrige, although it has been suggested that he was the member of Parliament for Derby who was imprisoned for offending Queen Elizabeth by presuming to discuss the question of her marriage.

Gifford Beauchamp Tower

'G G 1586,
Mala conscientia facit ut tuta timeantur. G. Gyfford'
(An evil conscience makes men afraid even when
they are safe).

The coat of arms and crest (*Argent, ten roundels*
gules, four, three, two and one, with, as crest, a hand
holding three gillyflowers) are those of one of the
branches of the very widespread family of Gifford. It
is assumed that they were carved by George Gifford
who is known to have been imprisoned in the Tower
as one of those suspected of involvement in the
conspiracy to assassinate Queen Elizabeth and so free
Mary Queen of Scots organised by Anthony Babington
in 1585–6. George Gifford came of a family which
had remained Catholic and his brother, Dr. William
Gifford, became a priest, later a Benedictine monk,
and, in 1622, Archbishop of Rheims. A distant
cousin, Gilbert Gifford, played a far more sinister
part in the Babington plot, acting as a Government
spy and, indeed, *agent provocateur* deep in the web of
intrigue which was woven around Mary Queen of
Scots' last and fatal attempt to free herself. George
Gifford however seems to have been a far less
effective, though not much more admirable,
character. About 1578 he was appointed a
Gentleman Pensioner, that is one of a band of
gentlemen who formed an aristocratic royal
bodyguard, and he remained one for much of his life.
He seems to have been chronically short of money:
in 1583 he went abroad and apparently tried to
persuade the Duke of Guise to support him
financially in an attempt on Queen Elizabeth's life.
When he was imprisoned in the Tower a list of
'articles . . . objected againste Mr George Gifford'
dated 13 December 1586 included five alleging
involvement in a burglary and highway robbery,
two for coining and one, included almost as an
afterthought, of connections with John Ballard, a
priest executed for his part in the Babington plot
and in whose company George Gifford had been

arrested. It is a little difficult to sort out his subsequent career: he was still in the Tower in August 1588 when the Lieutenant noted that he had been under his 'charge and custodie for two years' committed 'uppon suspision for diverse causes'. No particular punishment is recorded as having been meted out to him and he continued as a Gentleman Pensioner. A report among the State Papers, dated 28 May 1592, states that at some time in the previous five years the author had met George Gifford in Venice, returning from Constantinople; in 1601, Sir George Gifford was mentioned in connection with the Earl of Essex's rebellion and various letters among the State Papers between then and 1611 bear witness to a continued shortage of money on the part of Sir George Gifford, who in March of that year addressed a begging letter to Robert Cecil, Earl of Salisbury, complaining that he had served 39 years without reward. Finally, in 1613, a news letter addressed to Sir Dudley Carleton, the ambassador to Venice, mentions his death among various other general items of news.

The inscription below, also signed G. Gifford; '*Dolor Patientia Vincitur*' (sorrow is conquered by patience) is dated August 8, the day of his arrest.

Arundel Beauchamp Tower
'*Quanto plus afflictionis pro Christo in hoc saeculo*
Tanto plus gloriae cum Christo in futuro
Arundell June 22 1587
'*Gloria et honore eum coronasti domine. In memoria aeterna erit justus. A. Tuch*'
(The more affliction [we endure] for Christ in this world,
The more glory [we shall obtain] with Christ in the world to come.
Thou hast crowned him with honour and glory, O Lord,
The just shall be held in eternal remembrance . . .).
This is the most famous of several inscriptions carved in 1587 by Philip Howard, Earl of Arundel and Surrey, 1557–95, together with an inscription in his praise presumably carved by another Catholic who succeeded him as a prisoner in the Beauchamp Tower. Philip Howard was heir to the earldom of Arundel by right of his mother as well as being the eldest son of the Duke of Norfolk who was executed for high treason in 1572. As a young man he seems to have led the usual life of an Elizabethan courtier, spending money in what proved to be a fruitless attempt to become one of the Queen's favourites. He was however almost predestined by birth to become

the leader of the Catholic party and although he seems to have been brought up an Anglican, he became reconciled to the Catholic Church under the dual influence of his wife and of the writings and arguments of Edmund Campion. He was arrested in 1585 while attempting to leave the country and was brought before the Star Chamber accused of being a Romanist, of intriguing with Catholics abroad, of attempting to leave the country without the Queen's permission and of claiming the title of Duke of Norfolk on the grounds that his father had been wrongfully executed and that his title should not have been attainted. He was fined £10,000 on these charges, and imprisoned in the Tower. In 1588 he was further accused of praying for the success of the Armada and was condemned to death for treason.

He was however reprieved, but spent the rest of his life in prison in the Tower, where he died and was buried in the chapel 21 October 1595. His long imprisonment, and the austere way he lived while in prison, caused him to be considered a martyr for the Catholic religion, and it was doubtless this which prompted the carving of the lines in his praise, below his own inscription. The defaced signature may be that of Anthony Tuchiner who carved his name elsewhere in the Beauchamp Tower and who was imprisoned as a 'suspicious' man, 'a dealer with priestes', in September 1586 and ordered to be examined and 'put to the torture of the rack' in December of that year. He was still in the Tower in July 1588 but nothing definite has been found to indicate when or whether he was ever released.

Walpole Salt Tower

'Henry Walpole
S. Paulus, Petrus, Hieronimus, Ambrosius, Augustinus
Gregorius'

Henry Walpole, 1558–95, was an English Jesuit priest. He studied at Cambridge and Grays Inn before going abroad to train as a priest. He became a Jesuit in 1584 and was ordained a priest in 1588. In 1593 he was sent back to England. He was arrested in Yorkshire in the same year. He was moved to London and imprisoned in the Tower from February 1594 until March 1595, when he was taken back to York to be tried and finally executed. He has carved his name several times on the walls of the first floor of the Salt Tower, in one inscription adding the words *'Societatis Je. Presbiter'* (of the Society of Jesus, priest) below. In the example illustrated he has added the names of the Apostle who was a missionary *par excellence*, of the 1st Bishop of Rome and of the four fathers of the Catholic church, all saints to whom he presumably felt a particular devotion. These inscriptions are of particular interest because they are almost the only ones of which we have anything like a contemporary account. In his *Autobiography*, John Gerard, the Jesuit who was in his turn imprisoned in the Tower but who managed to escape, described how he was transferred from the Clink, the prison south of the river, to the Tower in April 1597. 'The next morning I walked round my cell. In its dim light I found the name of the blessed Father Henry Walpole cut with a chisel on the wall. Then, close to it, I discovered his little oratory, where there had been a narrow window. It was now blocked with stone-work, but there on either side he had chalked the names of all the orders of Angels. At the top, above the Cherubim and Seraphim, was the name of Mary, Mother of God, and then above it the name of Jesus; above that again the name of God was written in Latin, Greek and Hebrew characters' (*trans.* Philip Caraman, S. J., 1951). Obviously the chalk inscriptions have not survived, but the names of saints scratched below Walpole's own name presumably served a similar purpose.

Anon. Broad Arrow Tower, Salt Tower
'*IHS. MA.*'
A wounded hand. A wounded foot. A heart pierced by a nail.
These are further examples of the 'aids to devotion' carved by anonymous Catholics on the walls of many of the Towers within the Tower of London. Abbreviated versions of the names *Jesus* and *Mary* are particularly frequent, although this is an exceptionally finely cut example, but these representations of reminders of the five wounds of Christ from the Salt Tower and the Broad Arrow Tower are apparently the only ones to have survived.

Rookewoode Martin Tower

'Ambrose Rookewoode'

Ambrose Rookewoode, 1578–1606, was one of the 'Gunpowder Plot' conspirators. He had been educated in Flanders where his family were living in exile on account of their adherence to the Catholic faith. In 1600 he was allowed to inherit his father's estates in Suffolk. He became involved in the plot to blow up the House of Lords at the moment when the King was opening Parliament on 5 November 1605 and was captured along with others of his fellow conspirators at Holbeach House in Staffordshire. He was condemned to death for high treason on 27 January 1606 and executed four days later. There exists a romantic account of how he managed to say farewell to his wife, who was lodging in the Strand, on his journey from the Tower to Old Palace Yard, Westminster, where he was executed.

'The next day, being Friday 31 Jan 1606 were drawn from the Tower to the Old Palace in Westminster over against the Parliament House, Mr. Thomas Winter, the second brother of the Winters, Mr. Ambrose Rookwood, Mr. Robert Keyes, and Mr. Guy Faulks. By the way, as they were drawn upon the Strand, Mr. Rookwood had provided that he should be admonished when he came over against the lodging where his wife lay; and being come unto the place, he opened his eyes, (which before he kept shut to attend better to his prayers), and seeing her stand in a window to see him pass by, he raised himself as well as he could up from the hurdle, and said aloud to her: 'Pray for me, pray for me.' She answered him, also aloud: 'I will; and be

of good courage and offer thyself wholly to God. I, for my part, do as freely restore thee to God as He gave thee unto me' (John Gerard, *Narrative of the Gunpowder Plot*, ed. 1872).

There is an inscription by another of the conspirators, Sir Everard Digby, in the Broad Arrow Tower. This also consists of his name, without additions.

Peverel, Salmon Beauchamp Tower

'Peverel' and *'T. Salmon, 1622.'*

These are two of the most elaborate and most skilfully carved inscriptions in the Beauchamp Tower. They are both apparently signed and both can be dated (T. Peverel has dated another inscription in this tower 1571) yet it has not been possible to find out anything definite about their authors. None of the surviving returns of prisoners in the Tower made at or near the relevant dates includes either name and there is no mention of either in the relevant volumes of the State Papers.

From the dates it is possible to guess that T. Peverel may have been involved in the unrest associated with the Northern rebellion in the middle years of Queen Elizabeth's reign and that T. Salmon may have suffered from the revival of the persecution of Catholics during the middle and late years of the reign of James I. We have no confirmation of either conjecture.

The only possible independent evidence found for the existence of either is an entry in the register of the Chapel of St. Peter ad Vincula recording under the year 1626 'Thomas Samon buried ye XIIth of

September'. There is no note, as there often is, to the effect that he was a prisoner or any other indication of his occupation or quality. To add to the confusion, the arms depicted are not recorded as those of Salmon nor is the crest, of 3 intertwined fishes, presumably salmon, although it is a likely enough one. It is not clear whether the initials W.B. are a later addition or an earlier insertion nor whether the detailed account of the author's term of imprisonment 'close prisoner here 8 monethes 32 wekes 227 dayes 5376 houres' applies to T. Salmon or to someone else. The mottos '*Nec temere, nec timore*' (Neither rashly nor fearfully) and '*Sic vive ut vivas; et morire ne moriaris*' (Live in such a manner that you may live, and die that you may not die) are typical of those chosen by prisoners of a classical or philosophical rather than a religious turn of mind.

The Lord Mayor and Alderman Oliver in the Tower. 1771

Speech bubbles in image:
- We are imprisona for doing our duty therefore captivity is honourable
- Our Conduct is approved can the Ruler tell S. Stephens say as much
- CHARTERS of the CITY of LONDON MAG BILL of RIGHTS CHAR

Oliver Queen's House

'Oliver'

The eighteenth-century script makes it at least possible
that this name was carved by Alderman Richard
Oliver who was imprisoned in the Tower from the
26 March to the 8 May 1771. Born in Antigua in
1734, he settled in London and traded with the West
Indies. He became a freeman of the City in 1770 and
in the same year was elected Alderman of
Billingsgate ward. In February 1771 he and the then
Lord Mayor of London, Brass Crosby, became
involved in a dispute with Parliament over the House
of Commons' right to prevent the printing of
accounts of its debates. After they had refused to
imprison the printer of one such account, he and the
Lord Mayor were committed to the Tower for a breach

Published 15 June, 1771.   Bland Sculp.

By courtesy of Guildhall Library, City of London

of the privileges of the House, by order of the House of Commons. The case became a *cause célèbre*. Addresses in their support poured in from all over the country and the Speaker of the House of Commons was burnt in effigy. The engravings illustrated are examples of several that appeared during and after their term of imprisonment; in addition the portraits of both Crosby and Oliver, painted by R. E. Pine while they were in the Tower, were engraved and widely distributed. The two were eventually released when Parliament rose on 8th May: they were escorted to the Mansion House in a triumphal procession, and that night the City was illuminated to celebrate their release. This is supposed to have been the last time that Parliament attempted to restrain the publication of its debates.

Rickard Salt Tower
'*R. F. Rickard, October 1942*', kept up an old tradition.

Printed in England for Her Majesty's Stationery Office
by Brown Knight & Truscott Ltd.

Dd 289387 K240. 10/76